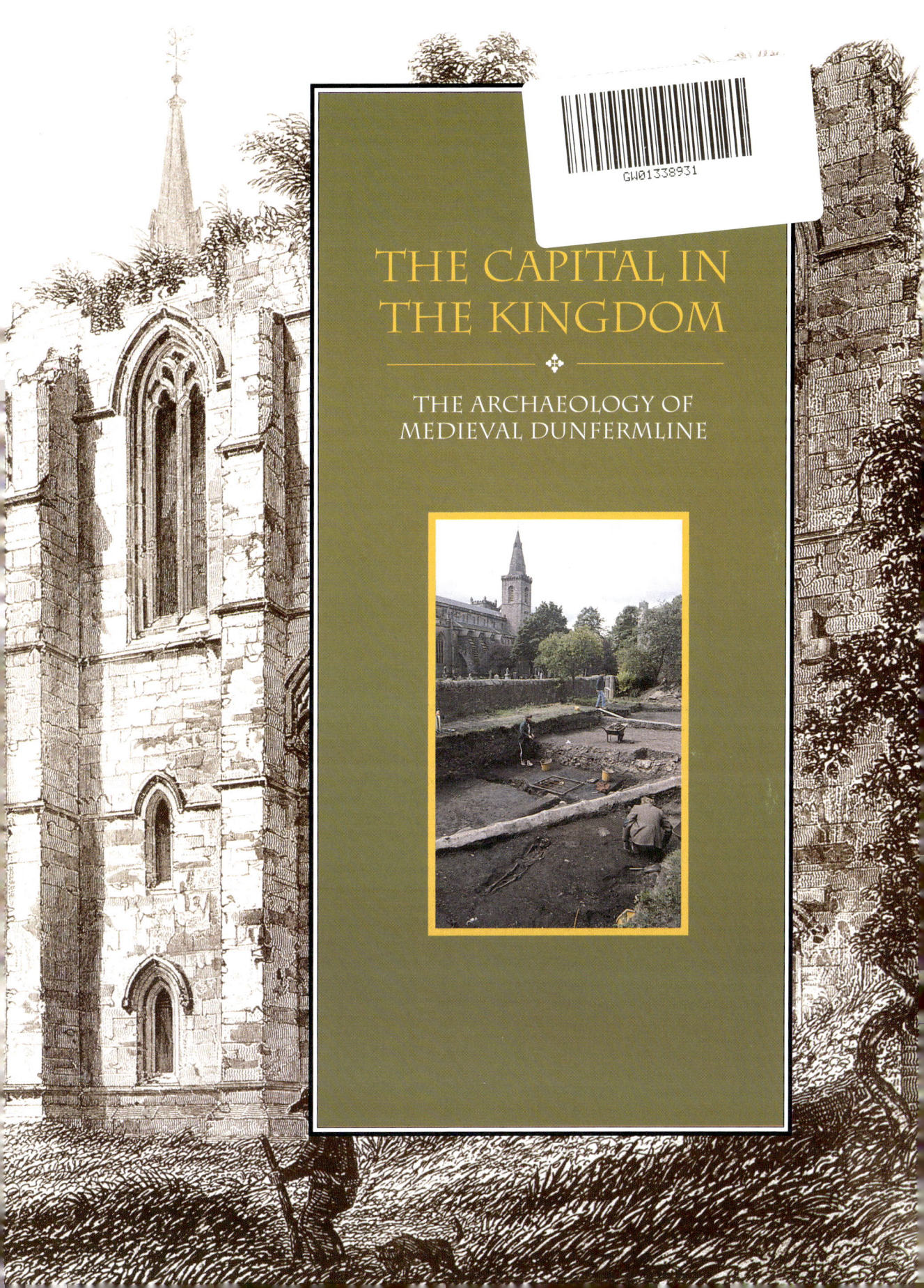

THE CAPITAL IN THE KINGDOM

THE ARCHAEOLOGY OF MEDIEVAL DUNFERMLINE

ACKNOWLEDGEMENTS

This book was written by Dr Pat Torrie (Centre for Scottish Urban History, University of Edinburgh) Russell Coleman (Scottish Urban Archaeological Trust Limited), John Lewis (Scotia Archaeology Limited) and Peter Yeoman (Archaeology Officer, Department of Economic Development and Planning, Fife Regional Council). Michael Donnelly (Dunfermline Heritage Trust) kindly provided the historical summary of the Abbot House which has been condensed for publication here. The book was edited by Peter Yeoman and designed by the Graphics Section in the Department of Economic Development and Planning.

The book was funded by Fife Regional Council, Historic Scotland, the Carnegie Dunfermline Trust, and Dunfermline District Council. The Regional Council is pleased to acknowledge support from the European Regional Development Fund to assist with the publication.

Fife Regional Council wishes to thank the following for their kind permission to reproduce photographs and prints:-

Historic Scotland (Crown Copyright) for Illustrations 4, 6, 8 and 10.

Sir Francis Ogilvie Bart for illustration 3.

Royal Commission on the Ancient and Historic Monuments of Scotland (Crown Copyright) for Illustrations 2 (inside front cover), and 20.

The Trustees of the National Library of Scotland for Illustration 14.

The Abbot House excavation illustrations are joint copyright: Fife Regional Council and Scottish Urban Archaeological Trust Limited.

The New Row excavation illustrations are joint copyright: Fife Regional Council and Scotia Archaeology Limited.

Illustrations 12, 13, 24, 26, 31 and 36 are copyright of Fife Regional Council.

©Fife Regional Council, 1994.

INTRODUCTION

History Beneath Your Feet

This book uses the results from the excavations in the Abbot House and at the Old Lauder Tech to illustrate how rescue archaeology can illuminate the lives of the people living in Dunfermline hundreds of years ago. This book is published in conjunction with the opening in 1994 of the Abbot House Heritage Centre, which will interpret the social history of the burgh, as never seen before, from earliest times up to the present day.

Until recently, few excavations had taken place in Dunfermline. These have helped, however, to build up a picture of where well-preserved medieval deposits do survive under the present streets.

In 1989 Fife Regional Council established the Fife Archaeological Service to help conserve the rich environmental heritage of the Region. One of the functions of the Archaeological Service is to monitor all planning applications to identify potential threats to the heritage. As a result more investigations take place and important archaeological information is now retrieved on a regular basis, with the results being added to the Fife Sites and Monuments Record.

Fife has the greatest density and some of the best preserved medieval burghs in Scotland. Some 25 of these have been given a special designation within the Fife Structure Plan to encourage preservation and, where necessary, excavation. These Archaeological Areas of Regional Importance include Dunfermline, and this designation along with the associated policies has helped enable rescue excavations to take place in advance of construction work. And so the Regional Council and Historic Scotland now require commercial developers to fund archaeological excavations on sites where developments would otherwise destroy buried archaeology.

But why are archaeological excavations necessary? Well, until the 19th century redevelopment simply consisted of levelling off the remains of previous buildings to build on top, thus encouraging the formation of stratified deposits, one on top of the other, with the oldest at the bottom. Modern building works are much more destructive, often involving deep excavations.

In 1992-1993 more archaeological work was done in Dunfermline that in any other burgh in Scotland. This work costing over £120,000, with very successful results, and prompted considerable public interest. The results are summarised here, preceded by an outline of life in medieval Dunfermline, derived from historical documents.

As develoment of the medieval burgh and historic royal capital continues, who knows what relics of the past await discovery!

LIFE IN MEDIEVAL DUNFERMLINE

he place name Dunfermline in ancient Gaelic means "the fort by the crooked water", the last part referring to the Tower Burn.

We first here of Dunfermline in 1067/1070 when the marriage of King Malcolm III (Canmore) to the Saxon princess Margaret was magnificently celebrated. Dunfermline was then termed an 'oppidum', which probably meant a small defended settlement. There is a tradition that King Malcolm favoured this spot, perhaps for hunting, and that he had built a residence for himself here. Whether this royal home was in fact the ruined fortified tower in Pittencrieff Glen, now called 'Malcolm Canmore's Tower', we can never be sure; it is certain that there was a royal residence in Dunfermline, and a settlement clustered around it. This was both for protection and for economic reasons since when the court was at Dunfermline the local people would find ready employment and a market for their produce and crafts.

Queen Margaret was to have a profound influence on Scotland, and particularly on Dunfermline. When she arrived there was nothing similar in Scotland to the type of religious or monastic life that was common elsewhere in western Europe. However, it was not long before she had brought monks of the rule of St Benedict from Canterbury and founded a monastery at the royal chapel where she had been married. By 1128, David I, the youngest son of Malcolm and Margaret, began the construction of a new and bigger church, and raised the status of the little priory to an abbey. So began a close and important relationship between town and abbey.

3: King Malcolm Canmore and Queen Margaret from the 16th century Seton Armorial

Although Dunfermline was one of the royal capitals of Scotland, life beside the abbey for the ordinary townspeople was simple. At the time of King Malcolm and Queen Margaret the small township probably consisted of little more than a huddle of timber huts, but sometime during the reign of David I (1124-1153) Dunfermline was raised to the status of a 'burgh'. As a burgh the town was given certain rights, including trading privileges, which were to bring economic advancement.

Photo 4: Dunfermline Abbey Nave, 12th century.

The town was granted the right to hold weekly markets and annual fairs, as well as having a monopoly on foreign and domestic trade.

By the fifteenth century, the time of the oldest surviving local records in Dunfermline, we have a fairly clear picture of what the town was like. To modern eyes medieval Dunfermline would appear to be little more than a village, with an estimated population of only 1,100 people in 1500. One thing we could probably recognise, though, is the street pattern since there has been little change in the central core over the last five hundred years. Running east to west was the Causagait or Hiegait (High Street), with Collier Row (Bruce Street) and Cross Wynd off it to the north. From the south side ran St Catherine's Wynd, with Maygate turning eastwards off it, and New Row, much as they are today. Queen Anne Street was in existence also, although called Ratton Row, as was Priory Lane, then Common Vennel, and Netherton.

Running back from these streets, were the burgage plots (rigs) of the townspeople. Dwellings were built at the front of the plots, and although there had been improvements by 1500, they were still quite simple. In 1624 Dunfermline was devastated by a great fire, indicating clearly that most houses were even then built of wood. By the early sixteenth century, most dwellings were roofed with thatch of cut heather or turves, and only two houses were recorded to have slated roofs. One of these was along the Maygate and may well have been the 'Abbot House'. If so, it was clearly a building of some importance. The exciting results of the Abbot House dig are summarised below, helping to clarify our understanding of this important building. Behind the homes the long rigs at the back were available for the workshops of craftsmen and for rearing animals and growing foodstuffs or flax. The records show that although Dunfermline was urban the atmosphere was green and rural, with animals, not only in backlands, but also often free to roam the streets.

There were some significant buildings in the town. Of utmost importance to any burgh was its market and associated tollbooth, market cross and tron (town weighing machine). The tolbooth was the most prestigious secular building. It was there that the town council met, the jail was housed, the market dues were collected, and the town weights were kept. The tolbooth stood facing up the Hiegait, where the City Chambers now stand. Along with the parish church, this was the building the townspeople provided most money to maintain. Unlike other towns, Dunfermline did not have a big, open market area or square, because of the lie of the land. Its market had to be linear and ran the length of the High Street with the market cross in its present position at the bottom of Cross Wynd. Dunfermline's market drew country people from a wide surrounding

5. Medieval Dunfermline.

area who not only had to pay for the right to sell at the market but also had to obey the rules and regulations laid down by the Dunfermline burgesses (the principal merchants) on matters such as the standard and price of ale, bread and meat: quality control existed even in the Middle Ages!

A stone gateway, known as a port, stood at each of the main access point into the burgh. The grandest of these was at the abbey, and is illustrated on the inside front cover. The gates were manned, and functioned to collect customs tolls and to provide security. Most of the ports were pulled down during the 18th century.

The building which dominated the town and surrounding countryside was the magnificent Benedictine abbey. The guest chambers, which became the royal palace can be visited in Pittencrieff Glen; this was where Charles I was born in 1600. Most of the abbey buildings were set within the precinct walls that ran along present St Catherine's Wynd, Maygate, Canmore Street, the back of the New Row burgage plots and Priory Lane, encircling an area of 22 acres. Excavations at New Row in 1993 focused on the buildings of the outer precinct. Although the monks and their servants were set apart from the townsfolk, the abbey and the several chapels in Dunfermline had a profound effect on the life of the town.

Dunfermline experienced set-backs, especially during the stormy Wars of Independence, when Edward I of England visited on a number of occasions. In 1303 he destroyed many of the buildings within the abbey precinct, sparing only the church. In 1385 the abbey was again burnt, this time by Richard II, who also set fire to the town. By the fourteenth century the superior of the burgh was no longer the crown but the abbot of Dunfermline. Precisely why or when this happened is not certain, but it was to be of the utmost significance to the town. Dunfermline, for example, was permitted to trade from the abbot's port of Gellet (Limekilns) - an important concession for a town with no sea harbour. The records show that Dunfermline merchants travelled not merely to nearby mercantile ports in the Low Countries, but as far afield as Danzig (modern Gdansk) in the Baltic, bringing home timber and flax.

The abbey gave far more to the town than economic advantages; it had a civilising influence on all aspects of life. Education was administered by the church, and the town was well endowed with three schools by 1525. We know little about them, other than that their main purpose was to produce choristers and educated clerics for the church. Some poorer members of society, however, did benefit from attendance at school and possibly from the teaching of Robert Henryson, the famous poet. In reality few children received a proper education as they were more important to their parents as a mini-workforce than as students and

6: *Dunfermline Abbey with back of the Abbot House behind.*

potential clerics. In 1433 when witnesses were required for an important enactment a small schoolroom was large enough to house all those who could sign their names. Another historical insight was provided in 1493, when the town common clerk of Dunfermline placed his signature in the Burgh Court Book. Beneath was the signature of his sister, Katherine Bra - perhaps the earliest signature we now have of a middle-class Scotswoman.

Provision for the care of the sick was minimal, but there were two, or possibly three almshouses in Dunfermline and doubtless the abbey provided a measure of solace and practical assistance. The best medicine often was self-help in the form of traditional medication brewed from herbs. Several diseases were rife, some endemic and chronic, such as leprosy, but medieval man was subject to many debilitating disorders, such as smallpox, tuberculosis, cholera and amoebic dysentery, as well as being host to numerous parasitic worms. This was perhaps inevitable where industrial and domestic premises were in close proximity in backlands. Animals were slaughtered and fish gutted in the streets; human and animal waste was left lying, and not always in official middens, with channels of water and gutters becoming open sewers.

The most feared medieval illness was plague. Scotland, along with the rest of western Europe, was struck on many occasions. There is a piece of interesting evidence about Dunfermline's attitude to the 'pestines' or plague. The town was not surrounded by high walls, but probably only by a simple ditch and pallisading. The ends of rigs formed the town boundary, and it was often a requirement that each tenant maintained the bank or ditch at the end of their property for defensive purposes. In 1444/45 Dunfermline decided that the town should be 'diked' (enclosed) in an attempt to keep out the 'pestines'. What is significant is that this was eight years before the first known national measures were taken against the plague and this must reflect the influence of the abbey.

Life was not total hardship. Holy days were days of rest, especially the feast days of St Margaret when large numbers of pilgrims were drawn to her shrine. Pilgrims brought wealth to the abbey and to the town - all had to be fed and accommodated in hostels and inns. On one Holy Day in 1355 the English soldiers besieging Lochleven Castle laid down their arms and joined the crowds in Dunfermline venerating the Saint, before returning to attack once more! Processions through the streets on saints days were not only occasions to honour the saints and display the banners

7: *A medieval pilgrim with characteristic floppy hat and staff.*

of the guild merchant and the crafts, but also a time for jollification with the people joined on the streets by jesters, tumblers, minstrels and pipers. Foot and hand ball were popular games, as were games of chance, all accompanied by quantities of liquor! In Dunfermline the townspeople could go to the 'buttis', near Lady's Mill, at the west end of Netherton to practise their archery. Plays were also welcome diversions. When Edward I of England came to Dunfermline in 1303/04 he was welcomed in the royal chapel by a 'boy bishop' - probably an actor in a medieval play. By the end of the fifteenth/early sixteenth centuries the townspeople were appointing one of their number to be 'Robin Hood' to act in the town play, and to lead the people in their May revels. This occasion was an important one, as medieval society was rigidly hierarchical - all had their due place, whether high or low, but in the Maygames the conventional order of society was inverted and high spirits prevailed!

8: Preparing meals in the Abbey Guesthouse Kitchen.

The life of the town revolved around the abbey. The outer nave, still standing, was the parish church of the townspeople. Here they maintained their altars with stone and wood carvings, paintings and rich furnishings, and listened to the preachings of the chaplains. Although the 'inner church' and the Benedictine monastery were somewhat cut off from the people, many of the Monks were the sons, brothers and cousins of

9: The Elder Carnival, 1559 by Pieter Bruegel.

Dunfermline people, and clerics were a common sight in the town. This abbey, classified as 'one of the major cultural centres of late fifteenth-century Scotland' had a far-reaching influence on Dunfermline society.

The later sixteenth century was to bring radical changes to secular values and spiritual beliefs. The status of the town changed when King James V granted it to his queen, Anne of Denmark, after which it became a Royal Burgh. The Reformation of 1560 resulted in the destruction of the abbey and the confiscation of its property. The guest range was transformed into a royal palace.

Even though Dunfermline had lost its wealthy monastery, it remained a popular royal centre providing a firm foundation for the development of Scotland's ancient capital.

10: The Royal Palace with Abbey behind.

INTERPRETING THE PAST

Archaeology is about interpreting the past to bring history to life. The importance of the excavations at New Row and the Abbot House was not in finding burials, or the medieval street or even the rare objects, but by showing how these areas of Dunfermline developed over the centuries.

All the work featured here has been done by professional teams, and as a consequence the projects are costly. Excavation is only part of the story - the work on-site is done very quickly to enable building work to proceed. Techniques have been developed therefore to allow most of the interpretation of results to take place afterwards, and this post-excavation work usually costs as much as the excavation itself. The total cost of the Abbot House archaeological project was in excess of £ 80,000. The Regional Council Archaeological Service acts to design the projects, and to raise the funds in such cases where heritage development is involved.

11: Skeleton record: Abbot House excavation.

During the excavations each layer of soil, skeleton, structure or cut feature, such as a pit or posthole, is described, drawn and photographed. All the finds associated with each context are recovered separately.

After an excavation has been completed, the archaeological evidence is sub-divided into phases. These highlight significant events or periods of use. For example, the construction of a building would form one phase, the demolition of that same building another. A new road or cemetery, or the shifting of property boundaries may also form key phases in the history of a site.

When all this information is drawn together with the results of the analysis of the artefacts and the environmental samples, a detailed picture emerges, encompassing everything from daily life to major historical events.

DIGGING UP THE ABBOT HOUSE

n December 1991 the Dunfermline Heritage Trust began to restore and transform the Abbot House as a major Heritage Centre for Dunfermline. Up until then the house was always thought to have been a 16th century town house built by Robert Pitcairn, Commendator of Dunfermline. Elspeth King and Michael Donnelly of the Heritage Trust, stripped away the modern interior and uncovered a previously unknown, two storey high, facade wall complete with decorative windows and doorways. This wall was set back within the present day Abbot House, and would have fronted directly onto the medieval Maygate.

One of the newly discovered windows caused great excitement. It is similar to those found in churches and abbeys, dated to the mid-15th century. This pushed the date of the house back more than a century. Could this building within a building have been the original lodgings of the abbots of Dunfermline Abbey?

The nature of the restoration work and the landscaping of the gardens prompted the Fife Regional Council Archaeological Service and the Heritage Trust to set up a programme of excavations. These were designed to identify the various phases of building, to help unravel the complex history of the Abbot House and its relationship to the abbey. Virtually the whole of the ground floor of the house was examined, along with one large area of the garden and the gap site to the west.

The excavations aroused considerable interest and were generously funded by Fife Regional Council, Historic Scotland, the Carnegie Dunfermline Trust and Dunfermline District Council, with grant aid from the European Regional Development Fund. The work could not have taken place without the encouragement and support of Elspeth King, Michael Donnelly and Margaret Dean of the Dunfermline Heritage Trust.

The work was carried out by the Scottish Urban Archaeological Trust between April and September 1992. The dig was a great success, revealing over 700 years of history on the site. The results of the dig and many of the finds will be incorporated in the displays within the Abbot House.

12: Abbot House: West Gable showing 16th century addition to north.

13: Unbricking of 15th century traceried window within the original north wall of the Abbot House.

HISTORY OF THE ABBOT HOUSE

Documentary research by the Heritage Trust has indicated that the name Abbot House given to the property does not appear before the 19th century. However, the setting of the house, at the junction between the abbey grounds and the town, would have been the natural location for the abbot's lodgings. Here the abbot would have administered the financial and business affairs of what was an extremely wealthy organisation, with one foot firmly planted in the commercial town and the other within the holy precinct. Research has also suggested that the house was neither built nor even owned by Robert Pitcairn as stated on a plaque by the main door, although he was certainly a powerful figure in the late 16th century.

The earliest documentary reference to the building dates back to the mid 16th century when it was in the ownership of William Couper, the Burgh Treasurer. The land remained the property of the abbey and the link here was through William Couper's brother, John Couper, a monk and lawyer. It was then sold on in 1550 to John Boiswell, sacristan, who had responsibility for the fabric and contents of the abbey church. After the Reformation the fortunes of Boiswell declined and on his death the house was transferred to his young nephew, Andrew Boiswell. The deteriorating condition of the property prompted his guardians to sell it in 1570 to James Murray of Perdieu. His purchase of the house appears to mark the second major phase of construction.

By the early 17th century the property was in the ownership of the Earls of Dunfermline, and referred to as the Great Ludging. Its thick stone walls and slate roof saved it when the great fire of 1624 swept Dunfermline. Financial difficulties forced the Earls of Dunfermline to sell the property in the late 17th century. Between 1672-1699 the house was rented by Lady Halkett, and it was here that she wrote her autobiography charting her extraordinary life as a herbalist, physician and supporter of the Royalist cause. In the 1770s, the property was in the possession of William Black, Clerk to the Admiralty Court. He was the last of the owners who significantly altered or extended the house from its original plan. Various outbuildings were attached to the gable walls of the property in the 19th century including a stable, a barn and a dairy.

14: Back of Abbot House c. 1856.

More recently the house has been used as a doctor's surgery and a temporary home to the Tourist Information Office.

15: Abbot house and the abbey precinct.

PONDS, BOGS, LOCHS AND DRAINS

he ground level in the garden was built up considerably during the Victorian period. This may have been done to cover up a complex of old and new drains which ran under the garden. The largest of these was a stone-capped drain or culvert that ran east to west just inside the garden wall. Historical records mention that the kirkyard 'was for the most part a swamp, and in rainy seasons it was in many places flooded with water'. By 1660, the problem was so bad that a fund had to be started to pay for 'a gutter under the graves'.

The source of the problem was the abbey fish pond some 200 m to the east of the Abbot House; easy access to a good supply of fish being an important dietary requirement of any monastery. Since early medieval times water was fed into the pond from the Abbey Mill Dam, situated in a boggy region at the north end of the town, which in turn was fed from the Town Loch. A small burn ran westwards from the fish pond through the graveyard to St Catherine's Wynd and finally down into the Tower or Back Burn. The overflow from the fish pond in wet weather was obviously too much for such a small burn and resulted in the continual flooding of the graveyard.

This network of burns and culverts served many purposes for both the town and the abbey. Firstly, the water was harnessed to produce a cheap and efficient source of power for the mills along the Tower Burn. Secondly, a complex system of secondary drains feeding into the larger burns and culverts allowed the townspeople to drain their homes and properties.

Lying at the bottom of a steep hill, the Abbot House was also prone to flooding. Excavations inside the house uncovered drains of all shapes and sizes running through virtually every room, carrying floodwater out into the garden.

16: Excavated stone culvert.

17: Excavated areas at the Abbot House.

THE MAYGATE - A MEDIEVAL STREET

Restoration work has revealed the original front wall of the 15th century abbot's lodgings, complete with windows and doorways, which would have looked out directly onto the Maygate. Excavations in Rooms 7, 8 and 9 and on the frontage uncovered the actual medieval street. Several road surfaces were uncovered, lying one on top of another, made up of small cobbles tightly packed together. The street was full of pot-holes and continued right up to the front of the wall. Vast amounts of rubbish was found, including broken pottery, rotting food remains such as animal bone and oyster shell, (in those days as common as fish and chips), wood and bits of leather, including an old shoe. It was normal behaviour then to throw rubbish out onto the street. In the warm weather the smell must have been revolting, and it was for this reason in medieval times that Canmore Street, at the eastern end of the Maygate, was known as Foul Vennel!

Under the Maygate

The abbey precinct wall was found below the oldest surfaces of the Maygate, and beneath the front wall of the Abbot House. A second wall was found 1 metre to the north, with a flagstone path set in the narrow gap between them.

This arrangement probably dates from the 12th century before the Maygate existed, when properties (rigs) originally extended southwards down the hill from the High Street right up to the abbey precinct wall. Historical records tell us that Canmore Street, east of the Maygate, was known in medieval times as "In Between the Wa's", a narrow passage between the abbey precinct wall and the garden wall at the end of the properties. Until now, this passage was not thought to have extended as far west.

18: 12th/13th century paved passage between the precinct wall and the end of the rigs.

22

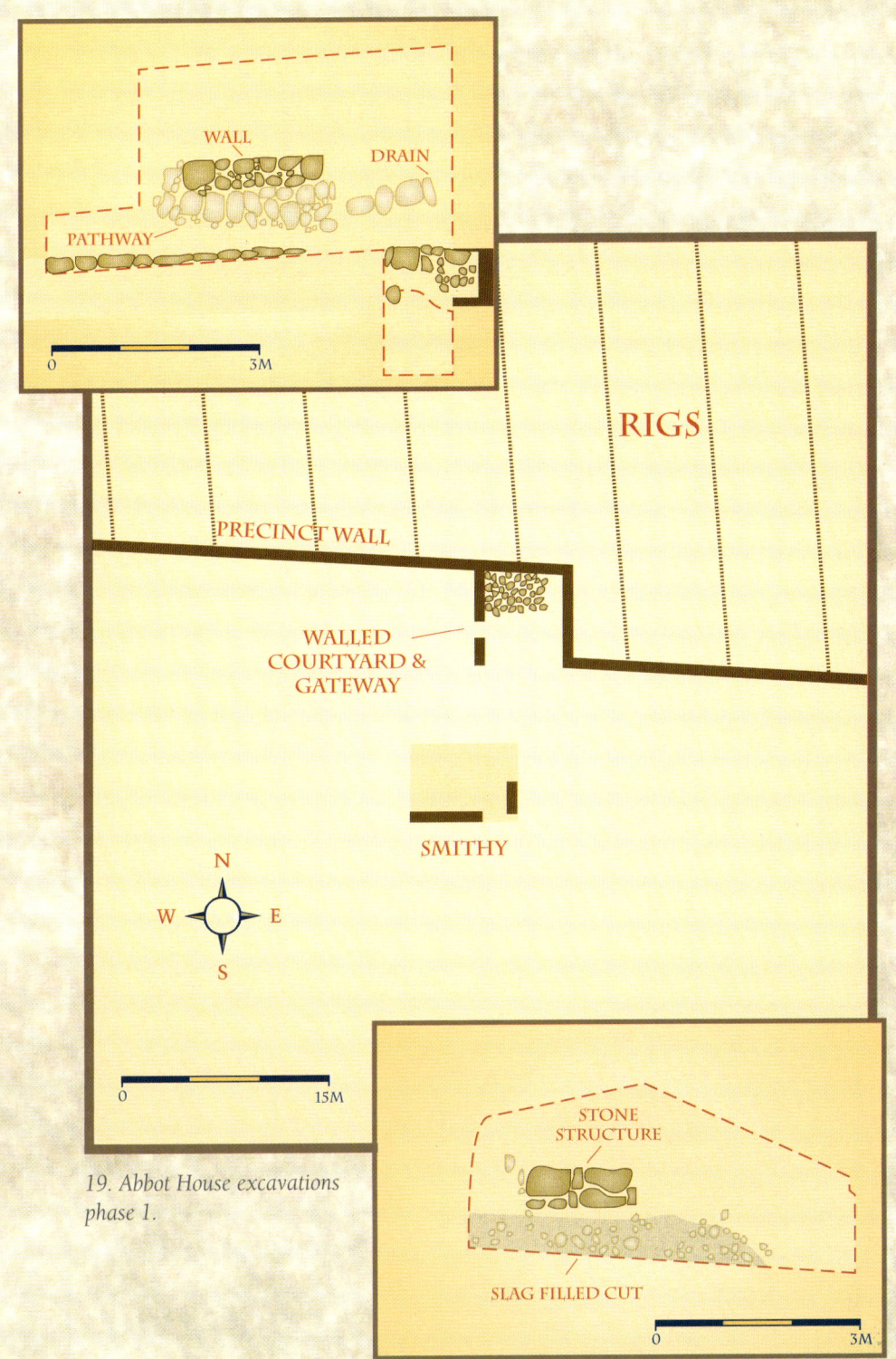

19. Abbot House excavations phase 1.

THE ABBOTS LODGINGS

he rooms immediately behind the front wall (Rooms 1.2.3 and 4) were excavated. These were originally part of the 15th century abbot's lodgings, but over the centuries alterations have obscured much of the detail of the layout of the rooms. Today these rooms are all roughly the same size and have, or had in the past, barrel-vaulted ceilings. When the floors were removed, the rooms were all found to be full of charcoal, coal, ash and slag deposits, and it seems that in the 19th century the ground floor of the house was being used as industrial workshops. A number of hearths and a clay, bowl-shaped furnace were also found, and probably represent the source of much of the burnt material. Unfortunately, this later activity has disturbed or destroyed much of the earlier archaeology.

20: Barrel-vaulted room under excavation.

Enough did survive to identify a sequence of floors, made up of crushed mortar and sand. They were not particularly hard wearing and were often repaired or completely replaced.

Courtyard and Gardens

Preserved below the mortar floors of the house were remains which pre-

21: Elevation drawin of a 14th century gateway from a building under the Abbot House.

24

date even the 15th century abbot's lodgings. In Room 4 a stone wall was found which contained two carved stone blocks, re-used from a window, and which marked a gap in the wall. A socket in the stones, probably for an iron gate post, indicated that this feature formed a gateway. This gave access into a cobbled courtyard. Before the abbot's lodgings were built this area was within the abbey grounds; if a courtyard and gateway once stood here perhaps they led into an enclosed area such as an ornamental garden, (see illustration 19 and 21). A similar cobbled surface was found below the mortar floors in Room 1, so it is possible that this area, was part of a courtyard or a pathway built against the inside of the precinct wall.

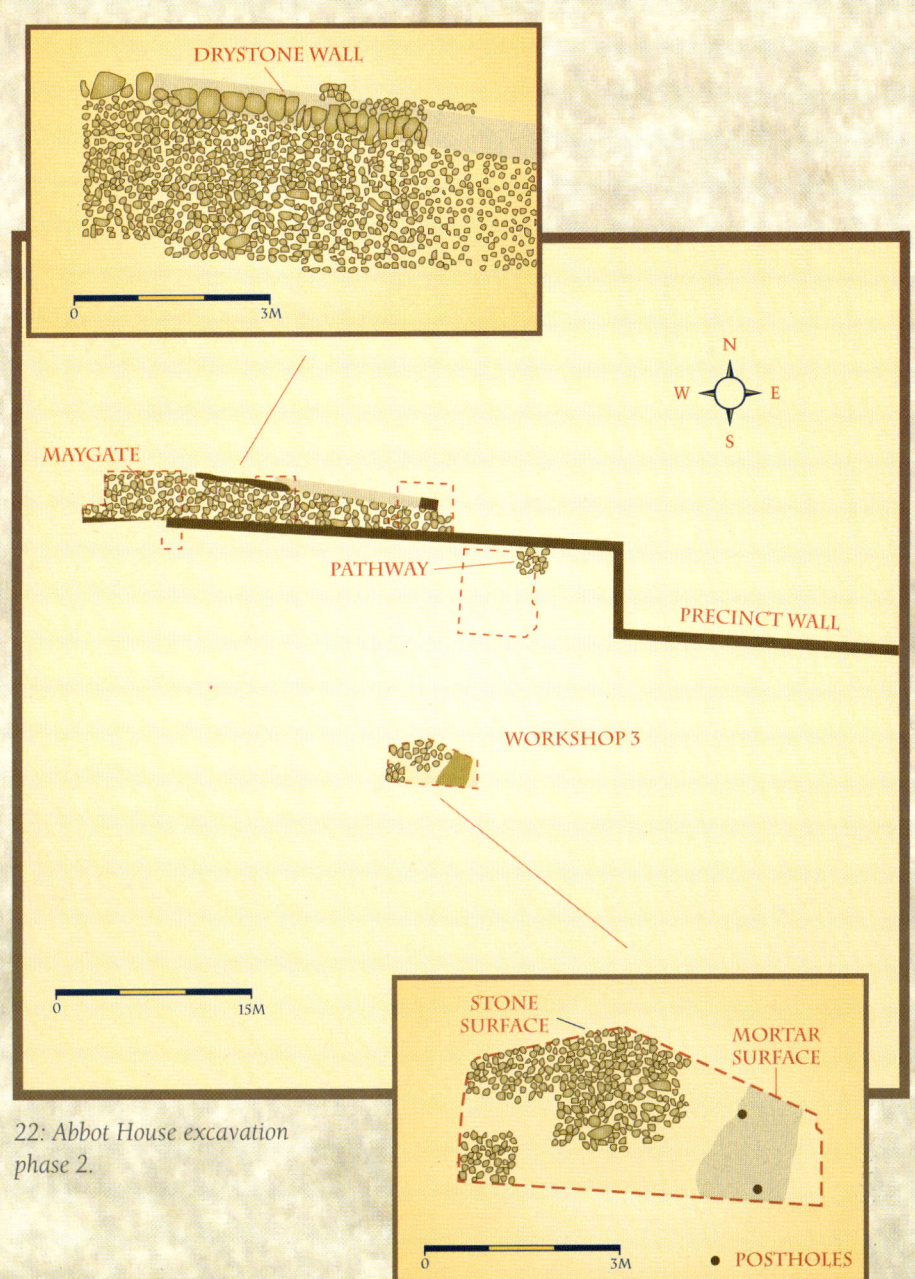

22: *Abbot House excavation phase 2.*

THE ABBOTS GARDEN - A WINDOW INTO THE ABBEY GROUNDS

Medieval Cemetery

An extensive layer of rubble was found under the garden, dating from the construction of the Abbot House in the 15th century. Once it was excavated an exciting discovery was made - it sealed a group of 10 human burials. So why were there burials in a private garden? Well, we now know from the excavations that before the abbot's lodgings were built, this area was part of the abbey graveyard.

The dating evidence from the pottery and coins found in the soils sealing the graves, suggests that the graveyard had gone out of use before the house was built. This area then became a private garden attached to the house.

The burials, both male and female, ranged in age from the very young, including a baby, to adolescents and mature adults. The bodies were laid in shallow cuts in the ground, wrapped in cloth shrouds. The material itself did not survive in the soil, but the pins which kept the shroud together did. One coffin burial was identified, that of a very small child, probably less than a year old. The wooden coffin had rotted away but the pattern of the coffin nails around the edge of the skeleton could still be seen.

23: 14th century cemetery under the Abbot House garden.

Sacking of the Abbey

One area, where there were no burials, provided an opportunity to look at what lay underneath the graveyard. Here, sealed below the graveyard soils was a thick layer of broken, worked sandstone, together with tiny fragments of stained glass. Could this be the remains of one of the palatial abbey buildings records tell us were destroyed by Edward 1 in 1303? If so, this is important in that it helps us to date the cemetery. As the burials lie above the rubble then they must be later in date than 1303. Therefore, the rubble layer gives the earliest possible date for the burials. We have already established that the graveyard had gone out of use when the abbot's lodgings were built in the later 15th century. Putting these two clues together we can now suggest that this area of the abbey grounds was first used as a graveyard some time after 1303, and that it went out of use in the mid-15th century.

24: Cemetery excavation in progress.

Smithy

A building was found sealed below the rubble. A sequence of clay floors and two walls defined a structure which may have stood here until 1303. The quantity of charcoal and slag that was found nearby suggests that this was a metalworking workshop. As a potential fire-hazard it made sense to have kept it well away from the main abbey buildings.

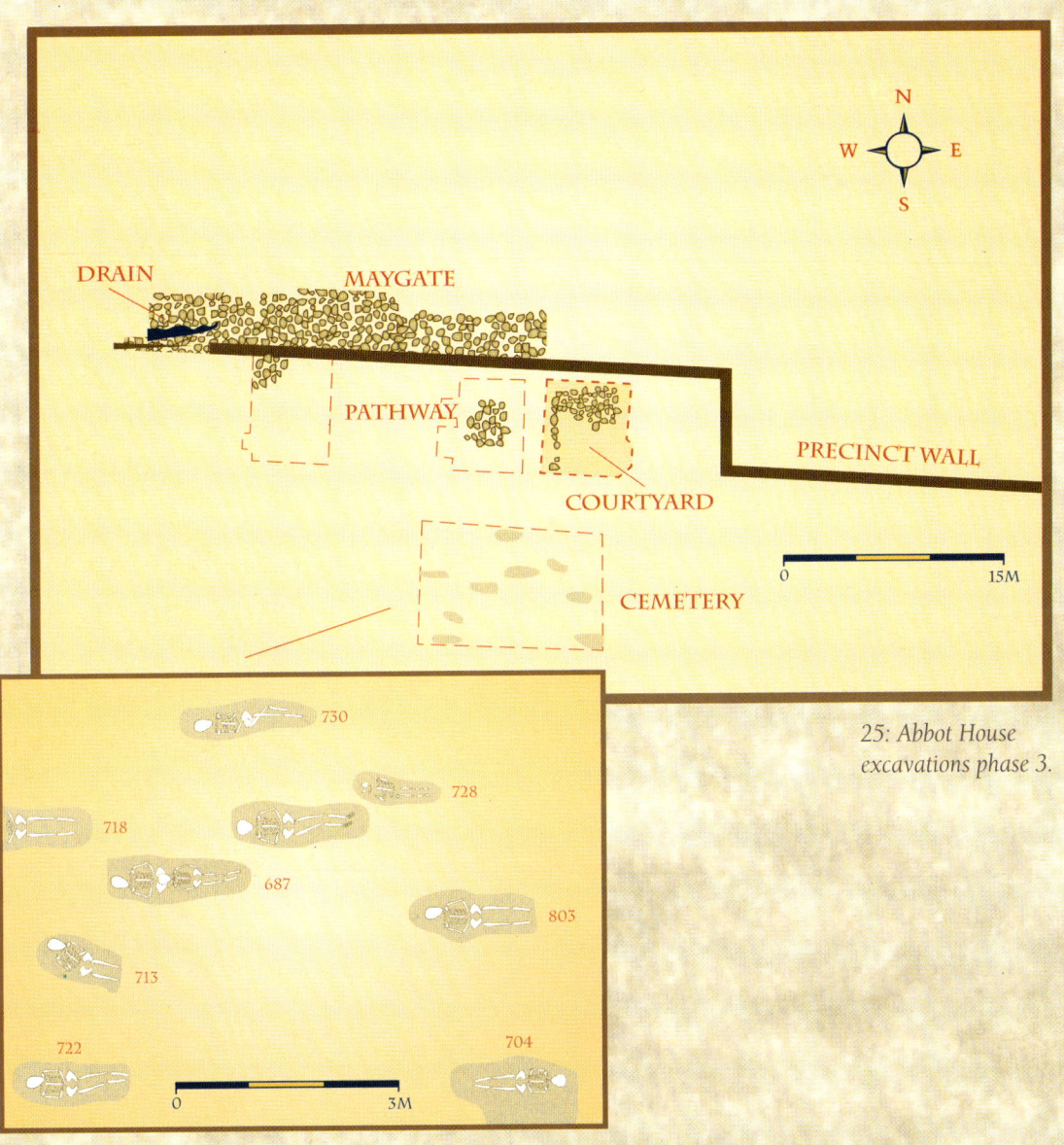

25: Abbot House excavations phase 3.

THE FINDS

A wide range of artefacts, made from different materials, were found during the excavations. Pottery and stone survive better in archaeological deposits than other materials such as iron and copper alloy. However, some metallic artefacts have survived in good condition, for example a small pair of tweezers, dating from the 13th or 14th century. This is one of the oldest artefacts found in the excavations and was found sealed below the cemetery. Other copper alloy artefacts found include a needle and several pins of different types.

One of the most interesting copper alloy objects was a small mount, originally from a book cover or a casket, found within the graveyard soil and decorated with a design of a female figure in classical dress - could this be a representation of St Margaret?

Coins often provide useful dating evidence in archaeological excavations. Careful examination of two coins from the garden area, for instance, gave a late 14th or 15th century date for the end of the cemetery phase.

Fragments of tiles, bricks, mortar and window glass, from demolition rubble deposits both inside the house and in the garden, provide information on the types of structures which previously existed in and around the site.

Some of the objects give an insight into people's daily lives and personal habits. An ear scoop made of bone, and the pair of tweezers mentioned above, may have belonged to sets of personal toilet items. Clues as to the types of clothing worn come from finds such as parts of leather shoes, copper alloy lace tags and buttons.

The finds also provide evidence about the tools and utensils used by people living in the Abbot's House. A whetstone for sharpening knives, which had been discarded in a layer of rubble in room 4, has a hole near one end allowing it to be hung on a hook or from a belt. Among the pottery assemblage were numerous fragments of a stoneware jug, dating from the late 18th or 19th century. This has been carefully reconstructed.

26: 14th century copper alloy mount with female figure(Saint?) 1.5cm long.

27: Coins including medieval silver pennies, found during the excavations.

28: Whetstone.

30: Reconstructed stoneware jug.

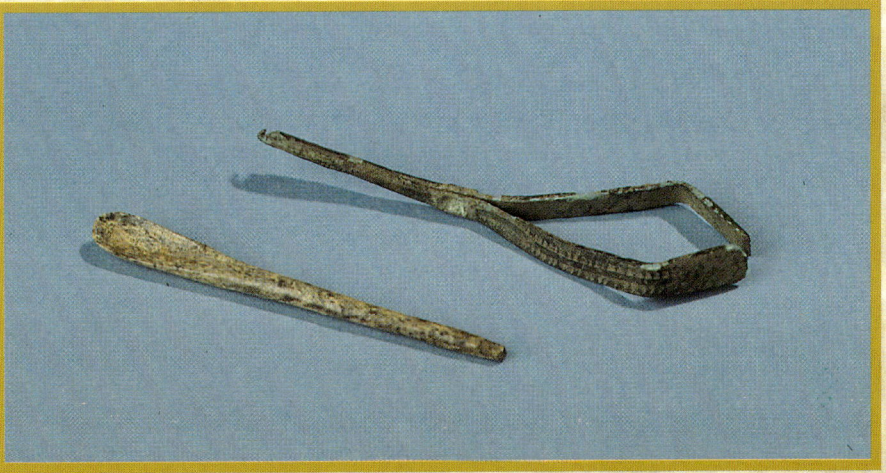

29: Tweezers and bone ear scoop.

LAUDER TECHNICAL COLLEGE EXCAVATION

In spring 1993 rescue excavations took place within the grounds of the old Lauder Technical College in Dunfermline, prompted by a major redevelopment programme. This site was very promising as it lay astride the suspected line of the abbey precinct wall. Any dig here could therefore provide information concerning not only the development of the outer precinct, where the monks and their servants had industrial, storage and other buildings, but could also tell us about what was going on over the wall, as fields were replaced by the growing burgh. The work was successful in revealing remnants of the 14th-century precinct wall and an earlier ditch - the same wall found in the Abbot House. Over the wall the dig found evidence of occupation on the outskirts of the burgh from the 15th century and of industrial activity from the 16th century.

Research has shown that by the late 15th century the burgh of Dunfermline was expanding with houses standing along the west side of New Row and plots laid out to the back of them. There was every possibility that demolition and construction work would destroy important buried remains.

The project was designed and managed by the Fife Regional Council Archaeological Service, and funded by the Regional Council along with Historic Scotland, Fife Enterprise, and the Carnegie Dunfermline Trust. Grant aid was also provided by the European Regional Development Fund. The time available to investigate these remains was at a premium: the demolition crew was almost ready to start work before the team from Scotia Archaeology Ltd could be mobilised.

The dig was considerably assisted by the efforts of Oliver and Robb, Architects, and WSP (Scotland) Ltd, Consultant Engineers. Thanks are also due to the contractors Nicol Demolition & Dismantling Limited and Bald Construction Limited. By excavating some areas in advance, and by skirting around the contractors' operations elsewhere, the archaeological team succeeded in retrieving a considerable amount of information without hindering the progress of the construction project.

The site was located on ground that slopes down to the south, about 300 metres from the High Street and 300 metres east of the abbey church. Buried beneath modern deposits of tarmac, rubble and garden soils, sometimes up to 1.7 metres deep, were the remains of two strong medieval institutions: the burgh and the abbey of Dunfermline.

31: Dunfermline Abbey and precinct with Abbot House to the left and the New Row excavation site visible at the top.

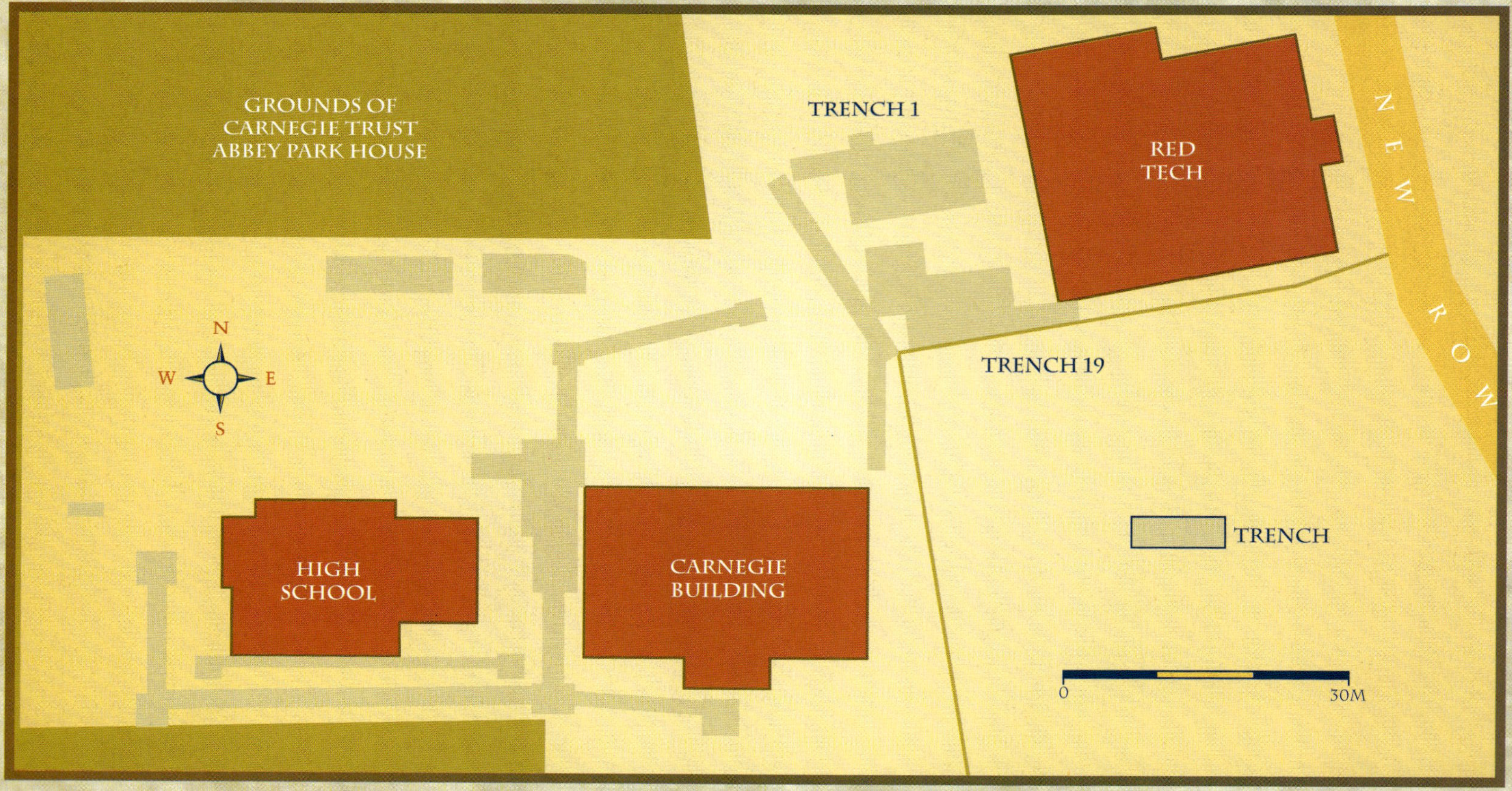

32: *New Row excavation trenches.*

THE ABBEY PRECINCT

The core of the abbey comprised the church and monastic buildings grouped around a cloister garden; the whole precinct was much larger and is estimated to have covered an area of approximately 9 hectares (22 acres). Near to the cloister, there would have been lodging houses, an infirmary and a burial ground; further out there may have been a smithy and other workshops; as well as gardens, orchards and a fishpond. All would have been surrounded by a boundary wall: at Dunfermline, these excavations have shown us that in places this wall was preceded by a ditch.

The excavation uncovered remnants of the precinct wall, the earlier boundary ditch, and the corner of a stone building in the extreme NW corner of the site. Although the position of much of the precinct wall was already suspected, its date of construction was not known.

The stretches of precinct wall uncovered were 0.9 metres wide and built of mortar-bonded rubble, standing to a maximum of three courses. In places, only the trench survived into which its foundations had been laid. "Robbing out" of stonework for new buildings was a common activity, particularly after the Reformation in 1560.

During the investigation of the precinct wall in Trench 1, the edge of

33: New Row: excavation of 12th century ditch with 14th century precinct wall in background.

what was thought to be a ditch was found on the west side of the trench. As a consequence, Trench 1 was extended to include the whole width of the ditch. This had to be done quickly: only a very short amount of time was available before the builders needed to work in that area. The trench extension was dug out, cleaned, its contents recorded and the trench backfilled within one day.

Although it was 1.7 metres below the level of the modern tarmac, the ditch itself was only about 0.85 metres deep. It was 2 metres wide at the top, narrowing to about half that width at its base. In all probability, the ditch functioned as a drain when it had lain open: it may even have been a stream bed - natural features were often incorporated into medieval boundaries.

There was a slight build-up of materials at the bottom of the ditch before it was deliberately infilled prior to the construction of the precinct wall. On the evidence of pottery within the ditch, this was done in the 14th or early 15th century. A rough flagstone path had been laid over the top of the infilled ditch, and this ran along the inside face of the precinct wall.

Building the precinct wall, which was probably a total of 1,200 metres (3/4 mile) long, would have been a substantial undertaking, even for such a rich monastery, and it is unlikely to have been built until most of the abbey buildings were standing. Being remote from the main abbey core, this stretch may have been one of the last to be built. Until that time, the ditch appears to have sufficed as a boundary. It may have been reinforced by an earthen rampart and/or a timber palisade -although no trace of either was found during the excavation. It was expected that the ditch would be encountered within Trench 19 but this did not materialise: perhaps its course changed towards the west.

34: New Row: excavation of abbey precinct buildings.

Limited excavation in the extreme northwest corner of the site uncovered the remains of a building buried beneath a mound of garden soil and debris. What was revealed was a corner of a stone building partly constructed with reused ashlar (finely worked sandstone) as well as unworked rubble. The quality of the reused masonry suggests that it came from a demolished abbey building of the 13th century, a period when construction techniques were of a high standard. At a later stage another structure was built against this corner, which appeared to extend under the grounds of Abbey Park House.

THE BURGH

ew Row was probably a thoroughfare from early medieval times, linking the town of Dunfermline to Inverkeithing and to the crossing at Queensferry. It is known that by the late 15th century burgage plots (comprising a dwelling house and small piece of land) were laid out on the west side of New Row as part of the expansion of the town.

It was also thought that these plots (or rigs) were laid out at right angles to the street, reaching as far as the boundary wall of the abbey, and this was confirmed by excavation. It had been hoped that some evidence of medieval housing would have been discovered when the 'Red Tech' frontage was demolished; unfortunately that building's foundations had destroyed any remains there might have been.

What was found, however, was one of the divisions between the backlands of medieval properties. Such plots of land were used for growing crops or for small cottage industries. On either side of the backlands division was garden soil containing much medieval pottery but very little bone. Such a scarcity is unusual as medieval gardens were often looked upon as repositories for household rubbish. Seeds of wheat and oats were also found in the garden soil, indicating that cereals as well as vegetables had been grown.

There was no trace of such a boundary in Trench 19 although there was abundant evidence of what can be termed industrial processes within one of the backlands. The discovery of the base of a kiln and its paved flue suggested that one of these processes was corn-drying. Samples taken from within the kiln contained many cereal grains, identified as barley and oats, as well as numerous seeds from weeds known to appear where crops are grown. Laboratory tests have shown that 11% of the barley seeds had germinated, a definite indication that brewing had been undertaken in this particular backland. The first stage of the brewing process requires barley seeds to be germinated and then roasted to form malt, an essential ingredient in beer making. It is likely that both brewing and the processing of grains into flour was carried out here on a small, domestic scale.

The analysis also revealed an abundance of burnt heather: this plant was probably used for fuel, and the kiln may have been roofed with it. A fire would be set within the kiln's flue from where hot air would pass into a circular bowl. Slats placed over the bowl would have supported a bed

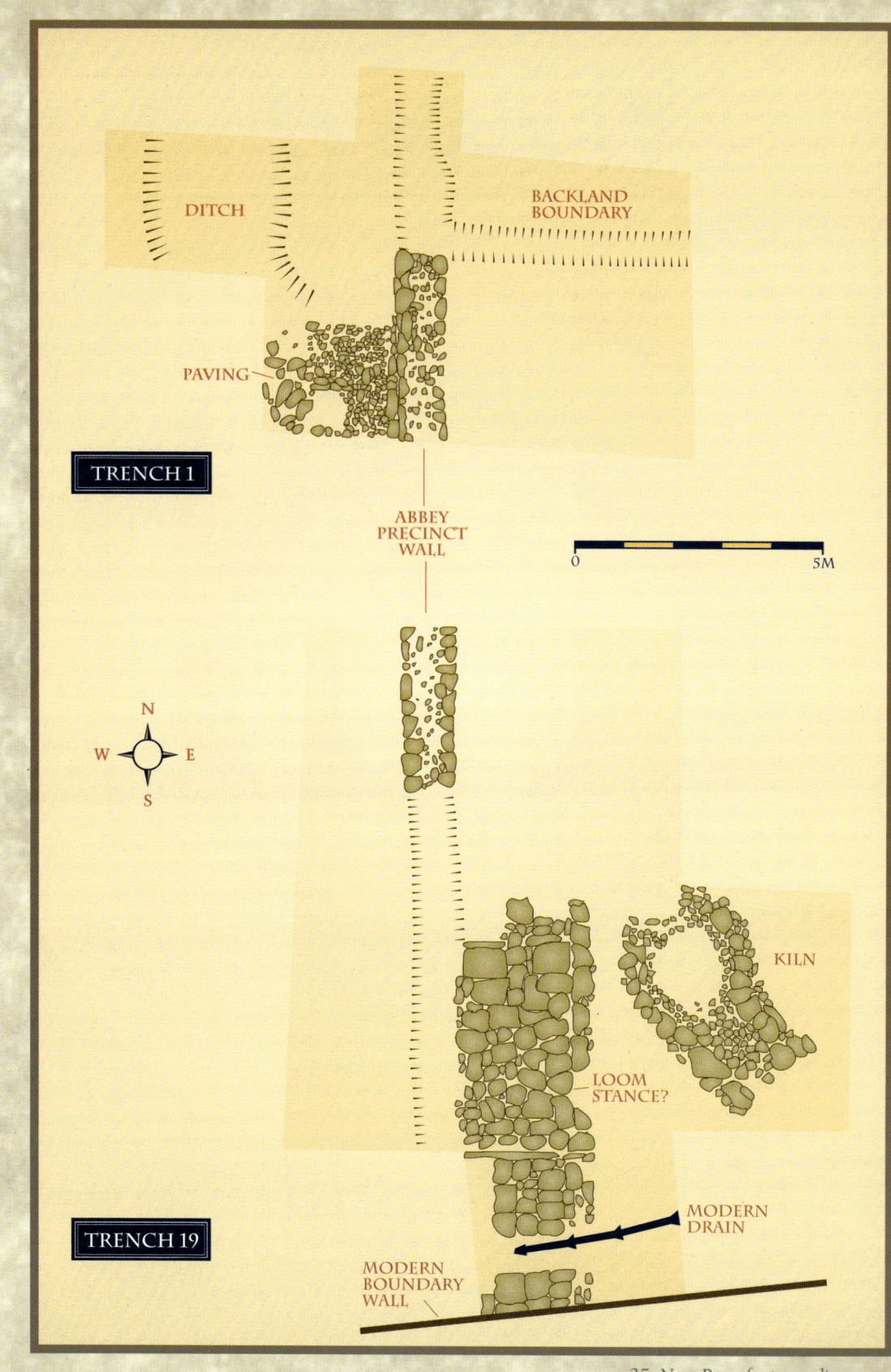

35: New Row: features discovered near precinct wall.

of straw onto which cereal grain would have been placed to dry.

Near to the kiln, and in the same backland, was another industrial remnant. A stone structure measuring 3.9 metres by 2.0 metres and floored with sandstone flags was built against the outside of the abbey boundary wall, set about 0.4 metres into the ground. Two stones sloped upwards from the floor on either side of a gap in the north wall. On the south side of the structure was a slightly raised platform sectioned off from the main floor by a short cross wall - perhaps the level at which people worked.

This may have been a loom stance, making this the oldest remains ever found of Dunfermline's textile industry. The town has had connections with processing textiles (canvas, linen and woollen cloth) and the attendant trades of weaving and dyeing since the Middle Ages.

An inventory of 1522 which lists goods owned by John Wilson, a bailie and dean of guild who held property on New Row and elsewhere in the town, included items associated with textile processing, namely *"ane pair of voll kamys* (combs), *ane kamenstock* (frame on which combs were fixed for preparing wool or flax), *ane spynnyn quhell* (spinning wheel), *ane voll creill, hekkils* (hacking combs), *kards* (instruments for combing flax or wool), *ane pair of woll shcheris* (shears)".

Pottery found below this small building and below the kiln showed that neither was in use any earlier than the 16th century. However, it is unlikely that they operated at the same time: the archaeological evidence showed the kiln to be the older structure.

36: New Row: Kiln and loom stance? in trench 19.

Although medieval backlands were certainly used for growing food crops including cereals (as indicated by the barley and oat seeds and by the presence of the drying kiln), some were also used to produce the raw materials used in textile manufacture. In 1496 a certain Thomas Bennis of New Row, Dunfermline, disposed of *"a loft and sellar witht as mekel of the yard liand tharto as a pek* (two gallons) *of lynget* (lint seed) *will saw"*. Such a crop could have been grown for two reasons - to provide flax (lint) for linen manufacture or to supply linseed for oil production. In medieval times the latter was used for lamp fuel.

There is no known reference in medieval sources to fulling or dyeing pits in Dunfermline although there are frequent mentions of tanning. The reason for this is probably because whilst textile production was relatively

clean, and tended to cause less trouble, tanning was very unpleasant and smelly, and caused many problems which required a documented legal solution.

Towards the end of the excavation, evidence was found of earlier activity under New Row. Just to the east of the abbey boundary wall, ploughmarks were cut into the subsoil, below the level of the medieval garden soil. As these small furrows did not continue to the west side of the abbey precinct wall and were aligned north-south at right angles to the backland divisions, it follows that they must have been cut after the wall was built but before the burgage plots were laid out.

37 New Row: Loom stance?

OTHER ARCHAEOLOGICAL WORK IN DUNFERMLINE

Most of the early archaeological work in Dunfermline was concentrated on the Abbey. The history of discovery dates to 1818 when the remains of King Robert the Bruce were exhumed during the construction of the new Parish Church. Excavations in the Abbey continued in 1916 when the nave of the St Margaret's church was uncovered, the plan of which is now indicated in the paving of the existing medieval nave.

Works took place around the Abbey Gatehouse in 1975 and in the southern part of the nave in 1977, under the auspices of what is now Historic Scotland.

Other than this the Scottish Urban Archaeological Trust Limited have carried out numerous investigations, all of which were relatively small scale. In 1981 works focused on the site of the new Kirkgate Shopping Centre, but little was found. The work on Canmore's Tower in 1988 was more successful although it showed that the site had been extensively disturbed in the 19th and 20th centuries. The ruins themselves were identified as being of a castle, but probably 14th century in date, the construction of which may have destroyed any earlier remains. Trial trenching in August 1990 in advance of the Central Library extension produced waterlogged organic deposits associated with the Abbey Mill Lade.

A constant watching brief has been maintained during pedestrianisation works, with the support of the Regional Council's Department of Engineering. The most recent discoveries were made during February 1994 in St Catherine's Wynd, where the remains of possible medieval stone structures were found 1 metre below modern ground level.

This work has served to show that in some parts of Dunfermline important, well-preserved archaeological remains await discovery, to reveal more of the mysteries of Scotland's ancient capital.

Historic Scotland is the executive agency within The Scottish Office responsible for administering the laws concerning the protection and management of ancient monuments. Historic Scotland identifies the sites and monuments that merit legal protection known as scheduled ancient monuments.

Historic Scotland also maintains and presents to the public over 300 monuments in the care of the Secretary of State for Scotland and is responsible for "listing" buildings of architectural or historical importance. In addition, it can provide general advice on the preservation and protection of ancient monuments and archaeological sites and landscapes, as part of its role to safeguard the nation's built heritage and promote the understanding and enjoyment of the heritage.

Historic Scotland has a "Friends" organisation; members have free entry to Historic Scotland properties and receive a regularly produced magazine, Welcome, which keeps them informed of Historic Scotland's work.

The address for further information on any aspect of Historic Scotland's work is:

Historic Scotland
20 Brandon Street
EDINBURGH
EH3 5RA